Fascinating

~Facts of~

New Mexico

Fascinating
~Facts of~
New Mexico

Aliens, Artists, Atoms

Marty Gerber

Terra Nova Books

SANTA FE, NEW MEXICO

Every effort has been made to assure the accuracy of the information in this book. If you notice that a particular fact needs correction or clarification, please email the information to info@terranovabooks.com. Future editions will be revised to reflect the updated information.

Illustrations by Andrea "Ani" Lozano

Library of Congress Control Number 2016960301

Distributed by SCB Distributors, (800) 729-6423

Terra Nova Books

Fascinating Facts of New Mexico. Copyright © 2017 by Marty Gerber
All rights reserved
Printed in the United States of America

Published by Terra Nova Books, Santa Fe, New Mexico.
www.TerraNovaBooks.com

ISBN 978-1-938288-71-5

For the three Gerber women in my life: Susan, queen of loving companionship; Barbara, invaluable co-conspirator in completing this book; and Jill, constant source of light.

Contents

Introduction 1

The Big and Little Screens 3

History 15

Geography 33

Cowboys and Indians 49

Arts and Entertainment 65

Science and Technology 75

Mas y Mas (More and More) 89

Introduction

WHO? WHAT? WHEN? WHERE? WHY? AND LET'S NOT FORGET HOW.

They're questions that can be asked about a lot of places, but few others have as rich a supply of fascinating answers as New Mexico. From a volcano you can walk into, to music from Holly to Dylan, to the hydrogen bomb dropped on Albuquerque, we've put them all together in this book for you now.

As might be imagined, it was a challenge to write—simply because the story of New Mexico, its people, and their achievements offers such a broad canvas of intriguing information to choose from. But we bravely waded through the annals of History, Geography, the Big and Little Screens, Science and Technology, Arts and Entertainment, and Cowboys and Indians to find the absolute most interesting facts we could—some of them already well known and others pretty hard to imagine.

We think you'll find a collection of learning and lore that will whet your appetite to know more about this extraordinary state. So indulge it: Travel our roads and rails, see our sights, read our tales, talk to our people, taste of our past and present. It's pretty easy to gorge yourself on the countless delicious slices of life baked into New Mexico's pie. But what a great way to go!

And in *Fascinating Facts of New Mexico,* you've got the ideal road map to get started.

The Big and Little Screens

1. Which native pueblo hosted the first film ever shot in New Mexico?

   Isleta, where the documentary "Indian Day School" was shot in 1897 by Thomas Edison on his recently invented Edison Kinetograph camera.

2. What 1940 John Ford drama of displaced Oklahomans making their way west to California was shot in part at Laguna Pueblo and in Gallup?

   "The Grapes of Wrath."

3. Which 1950 Golden Globe winner featured New Mexico's Carlsbad area and Carlsbad Caverns filling in for Africa's Sahara Desert?

   "King Solomon's Mines."

4. What 1952 drama told the tale of the kidnapping of a Los Alamos physicist's son by spies hoping to acquire the secret to the H-bomb?

   "The Atomic City."

5. What David Bowie sci-fi movie was filmed at New Mexico locations including Artesia, White Sands, and Fenton Lake?

   "The Man Who Fell to Earth," released in 1976.

6. Where in New Mexico was much of "Butch Cassidy and the Sundance Kid" filmed?

   Taos and Chama.

7. What classic novel, made into a movie in 1971, was set in the fictional New Mexico village of Corazon Sagrado?

   Red Sky at Morning, by Richard Bradford, who also wrote a regular column for *El Palacio,* the magazine of the Museum of New Mexico.

8. What 1954 movie, based on the 1951 strike against the Empire Zinc Company in Grant County, was denounced by the U.S. House of Representatives for its Communist sympathies, yet is now listed in the National Film Registry of the Library of Congress?

   "Salt of the Earth."

9. What 1969 counterculture movie that featured Peter Fonda and Dennis Hopper on a motorcycle road trip from Los Angeles to New Orleans had many scenes filmed in New Mexico?

   "Easy Rider."

10. What 1983 drama, based on the true story of a nuclear whistleblower and winner of five Academy Awards, including Best Actress for Meryl Streep, was partially filmed in Los Alamos and Albuquerque?

    "Silkwood."

11. The Western town set for which 1985 movie was custom built but then reused in "Young Guns," "Wyatt Earp," "Lonesome Dove," "All the Pretty Horses," and "Wild Wild West"?

    "Silverado," which starred Kevin Costner, Scott Glenn, Danny Glover, Linda Hunt, and Kevin Kline.

12. What 2005 drama was filmed in Silver City and told the story of Josey Aimes (Charlize Theron), a female miner who was sexually harassed while working at a Minnesota mine?

"North Country."

13. In what location are more films made than anyplace else in New Mexico?

The Eaves Movie Ranch, a Western town set eighteen miles south of Santa Fe, which has been the scene of over two hundred fifty movies and television shows.

14. Which Academy Award winner later became a New Mexico rancher and won championship ribbons for the pure-bred shorthorns she entered into cattle competitions?

Greer Garson, who moved to the Forked Lightning Ranch along the Pecos River after marrying its owner, Texas millionaire "Buddy" Fogelson, in 1949, seven years after her Oscar for starring in "Mrs. Miniver."

15. What 1989 road trip/buddy movie featured Philbert Bono (Gary Farmer) using his trusty steed Protector (a 1964 Buick Wildcat) to break out wrongly imprisoned Bonnie Red Bow from the Santa Fe Jail?

"Powwow Highway."

16. What northern New Mexico conveyance has been called "the hardest working costar" for its supporting role in movies featuring actors such as as Robert Redford, Paul Newman, Harrison Ford, Candice Bergen, Gregory Peck, Robert Mitchum, James Coburn, Kevin Costner, Dennis Quaid, Gene Hackman, and Sean Connery?

The Cumbres & Toltec Scenic Railroad, a sixty-four-mile narrow gauge railroad that goes from Chama to Antonito, Colorado.

17. What 1991 comedy, featuring four New Yorkers on their first cattle drive, netted Jack Palance a Best Supporting Actor Oscar?

"City Slickers."

18. What television crime drama series has New Mexico towns such as Las Vegas, Red River, Santa Fe, and Eagle Nest filling in for locations in Wyoming?

"Longmire."

19. Which Indiana Jones movies were partly filmed in New Mexico?

"Kingdom of the Crystal Skull" and "The Last Crusade."

20. Set outside of Taos, what 2005 drama starring Sam Elliott, Joan Allen, and a young Valentina de Angelis really *was* filmed outside Taos?

"Off the Map."

21. What film, produced and directed by Robert Redford and based on the book written by New Mexico author John Nichols, tells the "miracle" story of a small New Mexico town's battle against corporate development?

"The Milagro Beanfield War."

22. What 2007 Western, featuring Russell Crowe and Christian Bale, had the area around Santa Fe filling in for 1880s Arizona?

"3:10 to Yuma."

23. Although set in Marfa, Texas, what four-Oscar-winning movie, based on a novel by Tesuque resident Cormac McCarthy, was filmed almost entirely in New Mexico?

"No Country for Old Men," made in 2007.

24. High school students battled invaders from the Soviet Union (remember that?), Cuba, and Nicaragua in what 1984 movie filmed in New Mexico?

"Red Dawn," made in Las Vegas, in which Charlie Sheen and Patrick Swayze played brothers leading the fighting teen-agers in the opening days of World War III.

25. What 2007 John Travolta and Tim Allen comedy climaxed in a battle between two rival biker gangs in the town of Madrid?

"Wild Hogs."

26. What 2007 drama, set and filmed in Albuquerque and starring Tommy Lee Jones, Charlize Theron, and Susan Sarandon, gets its name from the biblical valley where the battle between David and Goliath is said to have taken place?

"In the Valley of Elah," a movie based on actual events that portrays a military father's search for his son and, after finding his body, the subsequent hunt for his son's killers.

27. Where in Albuquerque can the average person buy the blue ice featured as methamphetamine in "Breaking Bad"?

The Candy Lady of Old Town. (Note: This is rock candy, NOT meth!)

28. What 2009 romantic comedy starring Hugh Grant and Sarah Jessica Parker had various locations in New Mexico filling in for Wyoming?

"Did You Hear About the Morgans?"

29. Where in New Mexico were parts of the original "Star Wars" movie filmed?

White Sands Missile Range.

30. What 2011 sci-fi/western mashup featured Georgia O'Keeffe's beloved landscape and rock formations as the landing site of alien invaders?

"Cowboys and Aliens."

31. What 2012 movie that was filmed partly in New Mexico went on to become the highest-grossing comic book movie of all time?

"The Avengers," which has grossed over $1 billion.

32. What New Mexico native son has starred in such television shows as "How I Met Your Mother" and "Doogie Howser, MD," and movies such as "Starship Troopers" and the three Harold and Kumar films?

Neil Patrick Harris, who was born in Albuquerque and raised in Ruidoso.

33. What New Mexico astronomical observatory has been featured in Hollywood blockbusters such as "Contact," "2010," "Independence Day," "Terminator Salvation," and "Transformers: Dark of the Moon"?

The Very Large Array, twenty-seven radio telescopes located about fifty miles west of Socorro on the Plains of San Agustin.

34. What 2009 film about a fading country music star—partially filmed at Tesuque's Bishop's Lodge and in downtown Santa Fe at Evangelo's Cocktail Lounge—won Jeff Bridges the Academy Award for Best Actor?

"Crazy Heart."

35. What former high school thespian from Santa Fe garnered both 2013 and 2014 Best Supporting Actress Emmys for her role in a television series set and filmed in Albuquerque?

Anna Gunn, for her role as Skyler White in "Breaking Bad."

36. What 2014 miniseries that took us on a journey to the farthest reaches of space and time was largely filmed in New Mexico, including at the Santa Fe Studios soundstage?

"Cosmos: A SpaceTime Odyssey."

37. What 2012 movie, set in Los Alamos, was the first big-screen motion picture made from a book by beloved young-adult author Judy Blume?

"Tiger Eyes."

38. What do Santa Fe's Jean Cocteau Cinema and the HBO series "Game of Thrones" have in common?

Author and Santa Fe resident George R.R. Martin. The writer of the series A Song of Ice and Fire, upon which "Game of Thrones" is based, is also the owner of the Jean Cocteau. (Martin also serves as executive producer and writer of the HBO series.)

39. What Norse god was banished to Earth, landing in the New Mexico desert in this 2013 movie of the same name?

Thor.

40. Where can film aficionados go on the web to learn about the hundreds of New Mexico locations featured in film and television?

www.newmexico.org/true-film.

History

1. What state institution opened August 6, 1885 with a gala public reception featuring a grand feast, flowers filling its rooms, and lively dancing far into the night?

New Mexico's first penitentiary, on Pen Road in Santa Fe.

2. Who were the first Europeans to come to New Mexico?

Álvar Núñez Cabeza de Vaca and three other survivors of the Narvaez expedition, which was shipwrecked off Texas in 1528 while sailing from Florida to Mexico. The four men traveled through New Mexico and other parts of the Soutwest, meeting with many native tribes, on an  eight-year trek before making their way to Mexico City.

3. What New Mexico governor prevented a presidential impeachment?

Edmund Ross, who as a Kansas senator seventeen years before becoming governor, cast the deciding vote in 1868 against the impeachment of Andrew Johnson.

4. What is Blackdom?

Now it's a ghost town in southeastern New Mexico, but in 1901 it became a town established under the Homestead Act by and for African-Americans. Newspaper ads drew settlers who started shops and small businesses and built the town's population to some three hundred, but a drought beginning in 1916 forced them to leave, and by 1921, they all were gone.

5. **What was Lew Wallace's next job after serving as governor of New Mexico?**

U.S. ambassador to Turkey.

6. **What historic event is marked by Santa Fe's annual Fiesta?**

The return to the city in 1692 of the Spanish who had been driven out by the Pueblo Revolt twelve years earlier. Their return, led by Don Diego de Vargas, has been called a "bloodless" reconquest because no major fighting occurred, although isolated violence and incidents of insurrection continued through the remainder of the century. Spanish resettlement was accepted, however, because treatment of the Indians was relatively less harsh and their religion was given more acceptance and respect. The event has been commemorated annually since 1712 by Fiesta de Santa Fe, a multi-day series of religious and cultural events.

7. **What noted survivor of a New Mexico fire is often wrongly given the middle name of "the"?**

Smoky Bear, who as a cub was rescued from a tree he'd climbed to escape a 1950 fire in Lincoln National Forest. He recovered from burns to his legs and became a mascot for U.S. Forest Service efforts to prevent forest fires. "Smokey the Bear" sometimes was used as his name after the word was inserted in a 1952 song about him to keep the rhythm.

8. **What was the first incorporated town in New Mexico?**

Elizabethtown, between Red River and Eagle Nest, established with the nearby discovery of gold in 1866. It grew to a population of 7,000 but is now a ghost town.

9. **What was the Mormon Battalion?**

The only religiously based unit in U.S. military history. It was formed in Council Bluffs, Iowa, and marched nearly two thousand miles to San Diego in 1846 and '47 to join in the Mexican-American war. Though the battalion saw little actual fighting, it built a significant wagon road through much of the Southwest, and was guided across New Mexico by Jean Baptiste Charbonneau, who had been born while his mother, Sacagawea, was guiding Lewis and Clark across the continent.

10. What was the site of the only battle of the Mexican War to be fought in New Mexico?

Brazito, south of Las Cruces, where the Americans defeated a Mexican force on Christmas Day in 1846, and then went on to occupy El Paso before advancing on the city of Chihuahua.

11. The flags of what four nations have flown over the Palace of the Governors in Santa Fe?

Spain, Mexico, the United States, and the Confederacy (for two weeks). In addition, it was occupied from 1680 to 1692 by the victorious tribes that drove out the Spanish in the Pueblo Revolt.

12. What foreign general invaded New Mexico in 1916?

Francisco (Pancho) Villa, a leader of the Mexican revolution who raided the border town of Columbus on March 9 with 800 to 1,000 followers, probably because he needed more military equipment and supplies. His force set fire to houses and killed eighteen soldiers and civilians. A punitive expedition under Brigadier General John J. Pershing crossed the border into Mexico and chased Villa for almost a year, until the troops were called back because of the impending entry of the United States into World War I.

13. What New Mexico natural feature displays the writings of Native Americans, Spanish conquistadors, Anglo settlers, and many others?

Inscription Rock at El Morro National Monument, a sandstone promontory whose writings and carvings date back to the ancient Puebloans centuries before Don Juan de Oñate stopped there and added to them in 1605.

14. The tenure of what religious leader was marked by major cultural changes and educational reforms as well as conflict between native-born priests and European clergy like himself?

Jean-Baptiste Lamy, who arrived in Santa Fe in 1852 to head the newly established Diocese of Santa Fe. Policies such as the reinstitution of tithing, opposition to the Penitente Brotherhood, and appointment of priests from France and Spain created continuing conflict with local Hispanics. During the decades before he retired in 1884, Lamy greatly expanded the reach of the church and began construction of St. Francis Cathedral.

15. How did the Gadsden Purchase affect New Mexico?

It expanded the territory's southern border with Mexico by almost thirty thousand square miles, buying for ten million dollars all the land along the southern boundary of what is now New Mexico and Arizona from the Rio Grande to the Colorado River. A major reason for the purchase in 1854 was the acquisition of land for a railroad to the Pacific, which was completed in 1881.

16. How did the besieged residents of Santa Fe escape during the Pueblo Revolt?

By a nighttime attack on the sleeping Indians who had surrounded the city and cut off its water and food supply. Three hundred Puebloans were killed, fifty captured, and another fifteen hundred fled, allowing the thousand men, women, and children to abandon the city and escape south to El Paso.

17. What New Mexico road was renamed because of fundamentalist Christian beliefs associating the old name with Satan?

U.S. Highway 491 between Gallup and the Four Corners region, which was nicknamed "the devil's highway" when it was formerly Highway 666 (thought by some to be the "number of the beast"). One impetus to the renumbering was its high rate of accident deaths which led some to consider the road cursed—although higher-than-average alcohol use in the area could be a factor as well.

18. **What was the Santa Fe Ring?**

A powerful group of attorneys and speculators who became wealthy in the late nineteenth and early twentieth centuries through political corruption and fraudulent land deals. Legend has it that since they were all Republicans, the Democratic governor had Route 66 rerouted through Albuquerque instead of Santa Fe to punish them.

19. **Where in New Mexico were Japanese-Americans interned during World War II?**

Santa Fe and also Lordsburg, in the far southwest corner of the state. The experience for the detainees was far different at the two camps: Those in Lordsburg lived under harsh conditions and even appealed for help (unsuccessfully) to the government of Spain, which was responsible for enforcing terms of the Geneva Convention regarding treatment of prisoners of war. Operation of the Santa Fe camp, on the other hand, was relatively enlightened, with more respect for the residents' cultural heritage, to the extent that they were even allowed to celebrate the birthday of Emperor Hirohito.

20. **What was *El Crepusculo de La Libertad*?**

New Mexico's first newspaper, begun in Santa Fe in 1834. Its name means the Dawn of Liberty. (The first English-language newspaper in New Mexico was the *Santa Fe Republican,* which began publication September 4, 1847.)

21. What caused two small towns merge into the state's largest city?

The area of Albuquerque now known as Old Town was a farming community built up around a military garrison established on the Camino Real in 1706. But when the railroad came and put its passenger depot and railyards two miles farther east in 1880, New Town quickly grew up around it. The two remained separate municipalities until the 1920s, but once they grew together, the city just kept on growing, to the south, north, east, and currently far to the west as well.

22. Who was Doña Tules?

The operator of a famous gambling hall, saloon (and possibly a brothel as well) in Santa Fe in the mid-1800s. Born Maria Gertrudis Barceló, she often went by La Tules (a Spanish diminutive of Gertrudis). Although she was influential and respected in Santa Fe, her business made her notorious elsewhere— with varying and conflicting details about her life circulating widely. But on two facts there was agreement: her wealth and her skill at the card table.

23. What was the first major Civil War battle in New Mexico?

The Battle of Valverde, north of Las Cruces, in 1862, in which the Confederate army defeated Union forces and, despite heavy casualties, moved north to capture Albuquerque and Santa Fe.

24. **How did Las Cruces leap past neighboring Mesilla to become southern New Mexico's biggest city?**

After Mesilla landowners refused to sell rights-of-way to the Atchison, Topeka & Santa Fe Railway, Las Cruces, less than half its size, jumped at the chance and donated the land. Once the first train came in 1881, the city was on its way.

25 **What was the Organic Act? (Hint: It had nothing to do with food.)**

The law passed by Congress in 1850 that officially made New Mexico a U.S. territory and settled its disputed border with Texas. The first legislature that met under the act organized New Mexico into three judicial districts and nine counties.

26. **When did the United States take over New Mexico?**

In 1846, during the Mexican War, with the entry into Las Vegas of General Stephen Kearny, who proclaimed the people free from allegiance to Mexico, and appointed himself as governor. Three days later, on August 18, he peacefully entered the capital of Santa Fe.

27. **Who was Reies Lopez Tijerina?**

The leader of a group of Northern New Mexico Hispanics who raided the Rio Arriba County Courthouse in 1967 as part of their efforts to obtain title to about 2,500 square miles they believed were theirs under old Spanish and Mexican land grants. Although their rallying cry was "Tierra o Muerte," (Land or Death), they ended up with neither. Hostages were taken, though, and two people wounded, and Tijerina served two years in federal prison.

28. What was the first Spanish colony in New Mexico?

San Gabriel, across the Rio Grande from San Juan Pueblo, where the expedition of Don Juan de Oñate came to a halt in 1598. Being the only town, it was the capital of New Mexico until the Spanish decided in 1610 that Santa Fe was a better location. Most of the residents moved there, and San Gabriel was soon abandoned.

29. When did Shakespeare come to New Mexico?

In 1879, when two Englishmen decided to try their luck mining in the state's southwest corner and renamed the town that previously had been known as Ralston. They changed the old Main Street to Avon Avenue, and called the hotel the Stratford. But alas, the precious metals ran out in the early 1890s, and the Shakespeare Gold and Silver Mining Company was left with only a ghost town.

30. How was New Mexico affected by the Treaty of Guadalupe Hidalgo?

The territory reached most of its current size and shape with the signing of the treaty, which ended the Mexican-American War of 1846–48. Also transferred at the time from Mexican to U.S. ownership was all or part of what eventually became Arizona, Colorado, Texas, Nevada, Utah, Wyoming, Kansas, Oklahoma, and California.

31. What battle kept New Mexico out of the Confederacy?

Glorieta Pass, in which the South came out on top in the fighting but nevertheless had to retreat because a small Union force had meanwhile outflanked the battle lines and burned its supply wagons.

32. How did the first railroad crossing of Raton Pass on December 7, 1878 change New Mexico?

The territory was opened up to greatly expanded economic development. Shipments to eastern markets by rail created the great cattle boom of the 1880s, and its demise was quickly followed by rapid agricultural development. In addition, the easier import of mining machinery led to a major increase in the amount of ore that the trains then carried back out.

33. What was the Taos Rebellion?

An attempt by Hispanic settlers, aided by Indians from Taos Pueblo, to take back New Mexico from U.S. control after the forces of General Stephen Kearny occupied it in August 1846 during the Mexican-American War. In response to the rebels' killing of territorial Governor Charles Bent and other officials, Army troops engaged them in a series of battles across northern New Mexico, killing or capturing hundreds in fighting at Embudo, Taos Pueblo, Mora, Las Vegas, and other locations before the rebellion finally ended in July 1847.

34. What booming New Mexico city got its first boost from newspaper ads that turned out to be far from the truth?

Rio Rancho, whose nationwide marketing campaign in the early 1970s featured lush green land along the Rio Grande where only desert scrub actually was growing. After thousands of people had bought lots for "only $10 a month," the developers ended up in jail—a large part of the reason for the low prices that subsequently brought high sales results for homes and land there.

35. Who was "Uncle Dick" Wooten?

A former buffalo hunter who got permission from the governors of New Mexico and Colorado in 1866 to put up a toll gate at Raton Pass, the main Santa Fe Trail route connecting the two territories, and became a wealthy man as a result (aided by a saloon and lodging at roadside). He also "improved" the road, but it remained so steep, rocky, and winding that wagons needed five days for the twenty-seven-mile trip. Until the railroad bought up his right-of-way in 1880, every wagon had to pay $1.50, and mounted riders 25 cents, to get across the mountains. But Indians could pass free because local Utes had been his construction laborers.

36. What was the main industry at Carlsbad Caverns before it became a major tourist attraction?

Mining of bat guano, mostly for use as fertilizer, in the first two decades of the twentieth century.

37. Who did New Mexico support when the Civil War began?

Many of the early settlers who'd come along the Santa Fe Trail were Southerners, and thus inclined toward the Confederacy. But neither the North-South dispute nor the slavery issue were considered very important in New Mexico. (In 1861, there were twenty-two black slaves in the territory.) Popular support began shifting to the Union, however, because the first Southern advance into the territory was by troops from Texas, and Texans had always been disliked in New Mexico, dating back to their early desire to take over the territory.

38. What was the Rebellion of 1837?

An attempt to overthrow the newly installed governor of New Mexico, largely because of a fear of new taxes. The alcalde (mayor) of Santa Cruz formed an opposition government after a mob freed him following his arrest by the governor, who was killed a month later fleeing a battle near Black Mesa. But support for the rebellion began to fade soon afterward. That fall, the leader of a ragged rebel force marching on Santa Fe agreed to a truce in return for turning over the insurrection's original leaders, and the rebellion ended in January 1838 with defeat in a short battle near Pojoaque.

39. What noteworthy visitors came to Roswell in 1947?

Aliens from another planet, who were secretive at the time, and have remained so, about just which planet it was. However, it's known that they had a good laugh over the Air Force's initial story that their vehicle was simply a weather balloon, as well as over the official revision in 1994, which said the object that crashed was a balloon sent up to monitor Soviet nuclear testing for top-secret Project Mogul.

40. Where in New Mexico did the United States confine German prisoners even before entering World War II?

Fort Stanton, where some four hundred crew members of a German luxury liner were taken when the war began in 1939 and the British blockade of the Atlantic prevented its return from the Caribbean. After Pearl Harbor, security was strengthened, and hundreds more pro-Nazi German detainees were housed there. (Some 4,000 German POWs also were kept at nearby Camp Roswell.)

41. What was the Old Spanish Trail?

A trade route to California that began near Abiquiu Dam in northern New Mexico. It was established by Antonio Armijo in 1829, and crossed through Colorado, Utah, and Nevada before reaching the Spanish missions of California. The trail's heyday continued for about twenty years until traffic was lost to newer routes and ultimately the coming of the railroad.

42. What major route through New Mexico was created by Don Juan de Oñate?

The Camino Real, from Mexico City to Santa Fe, which was formally established by Oñate in 1598 although it had long been used for trade among indigenous peoples. The sixteen-hundred-mile route declined in importance after the opening of the Santa Fe Trail in 1821.

43. Who committed the famous Hillsboro Murder of 1907?

The killer was teen-age Valentina Madrid, who put rat poison in her husband Manuel's coffee for a week before he died. Also convicted of first-degree murder for helping her was sixteen-year-old Alma Lyons. But Valentina's "alleged sweetheart" at the time, Francisco Baca, who the girls testified had originated the plan and forced them to carry it out, was acquitted. After a public outcry over the young girls' mandatory sentence of death by hanging, the governor commuted their sentence, largely because of its potential damage to New Mexico's reputation and chance for statehood, even as the scaffold was being built. Valentina and Alma served nearly thirteen years in the state penitentiary before being pardoned (during which Alma gave birth to a baby boy).

44. **What opened up the Spanish territory of New Mexico to trade and settlers from the United States?**

The Santa Fe Trail, bringing wagon trains from Independence, Missouri, and economic expansion to much of the Southwest. Alternate routes took the trail from Kansas either over rugged mountains and Raton Pass or via the Cimarron cutoff, an easier way across the plains but with more danger of Indian attack. Established by trader William Becknell in 1822, the trail continued to be a vital route until the railroad came in 1880.

Geography

1. **What is the Jemez Mountains Soda Dam?**

   A unique geological formation near the village of Jemez Springs formed by the buildup over thousands of years of calcium carbonate and other minerals seeping from underground hot springs. The massive rock dam, named for calcium carbonate's similarity to baking soda, obstructs but doesn't totally block the flow of the Jemez River.

2. **What town built because its residents wanted to escape the United States ended up being part of it anyway?**

   Mesilla, created in 1848 by settlers who moved there after the Treaty of Guadalupe Hidalgo placed their former homes on the north side of the United States-Mexico border. But the Gadsden Purchase five years later added the Mesilla Valley to the United States, and the folks who'd moved there ended up being Americans anyway.

3. **What famous fugitives hid out in Whitewater Canyon?**

   Geronimo and Butch Cassidy (though not at the same time).

4. **What is the Los Lunas Mystery Stone?**

An eighty-ton boulder about thirty-five miles south of Albuquerque with a carved inscription that has been explained as a Paleo-Hebrew version of the Ten Commandments (possibly carved by a lost tribe of Israel) or an elaborate hoax, and many possibilities in between.

5. **How did the old New Mexico town of Hot Springs get renamed after a radio show?**

It volunteered in 1950 after Ralph Edwards said he'd broadcast his popular game show from the first town to adopt its name: "Truth or Consequences." Periodic attempts to revert to the old name have been voted down by residents who prefer their town's uniqueness.

6. **What saint is the New Mexico town of San Jon named after?**

None. It's a corruption of zanjon, meaning "deep gully" in Spanish.

7. **What New Mexico railroad line has a sixty-four-mile route that takes it over a ten-thousand-foot pass?**

The Cumbres & Toltec Scenic Railroad, which runs one train a day from May to October over Cumbres Pass between its headquarters in Chama, New Mexico, and Antonito, Colorado.

8. **What is the Malpais, and why is it so "mal"?**

El Malpais National Monument in western New Mexico is an ancient volcanic field of "badlands" (as the name tells us) filled with lava flows, cinder cones, caves, hoodoos, and other strange formations created over millions of years. It's stark, barren, fascinating, dramatic—and waterless. The area is so desolate, in fact, that it was a candidate for the Manhattan Project's first atomic explosion in 1945, but White Sands Proving Ground farther south and east was the ultimate "winner."

9. **What New Mexico city was named after three brothers?**

Grants, which began as a railroad camp in the 1880s when Canadians Angus, John, and Lewis Grant received a contract to build a section of the new Atlantic and Pacific Railroad through the area.

10. **Where is the Salt Mission Trail?**

It runs for a hundred forty miles in central New Mexico along the ancient playas and seasonal lakes southeast of Estancia that provided salt for the region's first Spanish settlements, and past the pueblo and old church ruins at the three varied sites of Salinas Pueblo Missions National Monument.

11. **What New Mexico city got its name because the river next to it was so loud?**

Ruidoso, on the banks of the Ruidoso ("noisy" in Spanish) River.

12. **What New Mexico mountain is the most southerly one in the country with an Arctic Alpine Life Zone?**

Sierra Blanca, ten miles west of Ruidoso, which rises to 12,003 feet.

13. **Where is the largest rifle range in the world?**

At the NRA Whittington Center near Raton, a thirty-three-thousand-acre site that offers hiking, bird and wildlife viewing, camping, and lodging as well as an array of shooting activities.

14. **There are very few volcanoes on the planet that you can walk into. New Mexico has one of them. What is it?**

Capulin, about twenty-five miles east of Raton.

15. **What New Mexico mountains form the southern tip of the Rockies?**

The Sangre de Cristos.

16. **What New Mexico shrine draws more pilgrims than any other in the country?**

The Santuario de Chimayó, with three hundred thousand visitors a year (thirty thousand of them during Holy Week). The church's "holy dirt" is believed by the faithful to have healing powers, and sometimes is taken by visitors hoping for a cure for their ailments. A room next to the little well of dirt contains dozens of crutches, canes, and walkers said to have been discarded as a miraculous result. The church takes dirt from nearby hillsides—twenty-five to thirty tons a year—to replace what is lost (after it has been blessed by a priest).

17. **What is the oldest continuously used public building in the country?**

The Palace of the Governors in Santa Fe. Built in the early 1600s, it served as the seat of government when the territory was controlled by Spain, Mexico, and the United States. Now a museum, it also is noted for the Indian vendors of arts and crafts who sell under its portal.

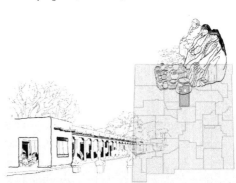

18. **North America's largest desert lies partly in New Mexico. Which is it?**

The Chihuahuan.

19. **What city has two streets named after the same person?**

Santa Fe, with both St. Francis Drive and San Francisco Street.

20. **What building has been described as the subject of more artistic depictions than any other in the country?**

San Francisco de Asis Mission Church on the plaza in Ranchos de Taos, a building famous worldwide for its massive adobe walls.

21. **How did Las Cruces get its name?**

The city, which has boomed into the state's second largest, came to be called "The Crosses" because of the many crosses erected in the area in memory of settlers killed in Apache raids.

22. **How did the town of Folsom get to be named after the prehistoric Folsom Man?**

It didn't. Things went the other way around. The Man was named after the closest town, and the town had been given the maiden name of President Grover Cleveland's wife, Frances Folsom.

23. **What New Mexico mountain is named after Giovanni Augustiani?**

Hermit's Peak, west of Las Vegas, where the Italian recluse lived in a cave he dug out of the earth around the time of the Civil War. Seeking more privacy from pilgrims who considered him a holy man, he moved his "hermitage" to the Organ Mountains of southern New Mexico, where he was found stabbed to death in his cave in 1869.

24. **Where in New Mexico do thousands of Boy Scouts come together for backpacking, camping, riding, climbing, and many other outdoor activities?**

Philmont Scout Ranch, near Cimarron, more than two hundred square miles of rugged wilderness offering adventure outings for youths and training for adult leaders.

25. **What Santa Fe building is the largest adobe structure in the country?**

Cristo Rey Church.

26. **What famous ancient homes are said to have been found because of an attempt to avoid jury duty?**

The Mogollons' Gila Cliff Dwellings north of Silver City, first spotted by a non-Indian in 1878 when Henry Ailman went into the mountains on a prospecting trip along with some friends who also were on a jury list and didn't want to be called to serve.

27. **How did the Organ Mountains get their name?**

From their similar appearance to organ pipes, especially in the granite "needles" in the highest part of the range.

28. **What high mountain retreat offered a relaxing respite for Al Capone, Pancho Villa, and Judy Garland?**

The Lodge at Cloudcroft, nine thousand feet up in southern New Mexico's Sacramento Mountains.

29. What mountain ranges named after fruits have a canyon that cuts between them?

The Sandia (watermelon) and Manzano (apple) mountains, separated by Tijeras (scissors) Canyon.

30. For what nineteenth-century building was a "miracle" needed to correct an architect's mistake?

The Loretto Chapel in Santa Fe, where the lack of a staircase to the choir loft was realized only when construction was almost complete. Since there was no room for a standard staircase, the Sisters of Loretto, whose convent it served, prayed for help to St. Joseph. Seemingly in response, a stranger appeared and, working alone with only primitive tools, built a spiral staircase. Then he was gone. The nuns believed the woodworker was the saint himself (though others have credited a French carpenter living in Santa Fe at the time).

31. What famous outlaws are known to have taken a break from fleeing the law at Montezuma Hot Springs?

Jesse James and Billy the Kid.

32. What extinct volcanic shield in New Mexico is the largest single mountain in North America when measured around its base?

Sierra Grande, ten miles southeast of Folsom in Union County. At 8,720 feet, it is the easternmost point in the country higher than 8,000 feet.

33. What little New Mexico town had the first baseball park with lights west of the Mississippi?

Madrid (accent on the first syllable in the local lingo), which now attracts tourists for its arts and crafts but was a busy coal mining community in the 1920s when mine owner Oscar Huber built the ballpark (now named for him) so his workers could have a place to play.

34. What does the blood of Christ have to do with New Mexico's highest mountains?

The name of the Sangre de Cristo range comes from the reddish color sometimes caused by alpenglow and seen in the mountains at sunrise or sunset. It was not bestowed by the state's Spanish settlers, though, since before the early nineteenth century, the mountains generally were referred to as the Sierra Nevada or Sierra Madre.

35. What are the Staked Plains?

The Llano Estacado (sometimes translated as Stockaded Plains) is a thirty-thousand-square-mile plateau of high plains in eastern New Mexico. The likeliest theory is that the mesa, one of North America's largest, got its name from the fortress-like appearance of steep cliffs along its edges, although some say it came from the stakes Spanish explorers drove into the ground to help guide them across the flat, featureless grasslands.

36. Where is New Mexico's largest lake?

Elephant Butte, about six miles north of Truth or Consequences. The forty-mile-long reservoir, created by damming the Rio Grande for electric power and irrigation, is named after the shape of a volcanic core sitting in the middle. The lake is one of the very few places in the state where you can sometimes see pelicans.

37. What New Mexico area is famous for having a "racecourse" and a "box"?

The Rio Grande Gorge, where those two sections of the river are the state's most popular for whitewater rafting and kayaking.

38. **Where does a nineteenth-century, water-powered flour mill still run as part of a museum exhibit recalling the importance of wheat farming and milling to the economy of northeastern New Mexico?**

The town of Cleveland, in Mora County, where the three-story adobe Roller Mill Museum shows off its intact and operable original equipment and holds the Cleveland Millfest every Labor Day weekend.

39. **What New Mexico site whose visitors have included Theodore Roosevelt, Jesse James, and Emperor Hirohito of Japan now has hundreds of youths from all over the world living and studying there?**

Armand Hammer United World College of the American West, in Montezuma. The school is part of the United World College movement which is aimed at contributing to international understanding by overcoming religious, cultural, and racial misconceptions among young people. It is housed in the former Montezuma Castle, originally a four-hundred-room luxury resort.

40. **Where is Chance City?**

About halfway between Deming and Lordsburg in southern New Mexico. The town considered itself lucky when gold, silver, and other metals were found in the nearby Victorio Mountains in the 1880s. But the wheel of fate made it a loser when only about half a million dollars worth could be extracted, and today just a few building foundations, scattered debris, and boarded up shafts are left. The town's most famous mine owner, William Randolph Hearst, went on to many more-fortunate opportunities despite the fact that he'd named his dig there the Last Chance.

41. **What are the four New Mexico towns with three-letter names?**

Abo, Lea, Roy, and Jal (whose name is an acronym for rancher John A. Lynch).

42. **What New Mexico town is named after the first king of France?**

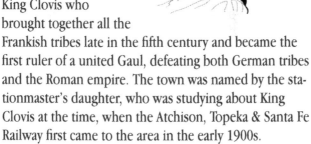

Clovis, named after King Clovis who brought together all the Frankish tribes late in the fifth century and became the first ruler of a united Gaul, defeating both German tribes and the Roman empire. The town was named by the stationmaster's daughter, who was studying about King Clovis at the time, when the Atchison, Topeka & Santa Fe Railway first came to the area in the early 1900s.

Cowboys and
Indians

1. **What happened on the Goodnight-Loving Trail?**

Cattle moved—and moved and moved and moved. After blazing the trail in 1866, Charles Goodnight and his partner, Oliver Loving, brought fifteen hundred head up from Texas to sell in New Mexico and Colorado (a two-thousand-mile journey for which Goodnight invented the chuckwagon). After Loving died the next year, Goodnight joined with New Mexico rancher John Chisum to keep driving herds from Texas and southern New Mexico up to Colorado and Wyoming until the railroad came and took their business away in the early 1880s.

2. **What did Jack Ketchum do for a living?**

He robbed trains. After killing several people in three train robberies and other crimes, "Black Jack" Ketchum was wounded robbing another and captured soon afterward. His injury resulted in amputation of his arm, and his hanging, in 1901, resulted in his decapitation.

3. **What language do New Mexico's Pueblo Indians speak?**

There are three language groupings: Keresan (spoken in the Pueblos of Acoma, Laguna, Cochiti, San Felipe, Santa Ana, Zia, and Kewa—which was called Santo Domingo until 2009); Tewa (the Pueblos of Nambé, Pojoaque, San Ildefonso, Santa Clara, Tesuque, and Ohkay Owingeh—formerly San Juan); and Tiwa (Picuris, Taos, Sandia, Isleta, and Ysleta del Sur—a Pueblo that actually is in El Paso County, Texas). In addition, Towa is spoken at Jemez Pueblo, and Zunian at Zuni Pueblo.

4. **Who starved at Starvation Peak?**

That depends on which legend you believe. The two top candidates are Spanish colonists or travelers centuries later on the nearby Santa Fe Trail. In either case, the stories seem to agree that they were chased up there by local Indians and came to an unhappy and hungry end.

5. **Who was Elfego Baca?**

A New Mexico gunman who always wanted to be a lawman.  In 1884, at age nineteen, he stole some guns, bought a mail-order sheriff's badge, and made himself a deputy sheriff in Socorro County, later becoming sheriff and a U.S. marshal. After a few years of arresting—or killing—local lawbreakers, he became a lawyer and served afterward as county clerk, mayor, school superintendent, and district attorney in Socorro.

6. **What are kachinas?**

Kachinas (also spelled "katsinas") are spirits in the culture and religion of many Pueblo peoples. They are considered powerful forces although they are not worshipped in the same sense as a god. Wooden figures representing any of the hundreds of kachinas are "kachina dolls," and tribal members who dress as kachinas for religious ceremonies are "kachina dancers."

7. **The country's largest Indian reservation is partly in New Mexico. What tribe lives there?**

The Navajo, whose twenty-seven-thousand-square-mile reservation covers large portions of Arizona as well. One third of Navajo Nation residents live in New Mexico.

8. **What tribe do most other Indians in the state belong to?**

Most other natives in the state are Pueblo Indians, although this is not actually a tribe. They reflect different physical strains and admixtures even though the early Spanish explorers thought of them as a tribe because they shared cultural similarities and common patterns of communal living. Each of the nineteen New Mexico Pueblos is independent, although an umbrella organization, the All Indian Pueblo Council, administers social services programs for the Pueblos.

9. **What branch of the Mogollon people built pueblo villages with as many as two hundred rooms and became noted for the patterns of their distinctive black-on-white pottery?**

The Mimbres culture, whose members lived in hundreds of small villages in southern New Mexico from about A.D. 100 to 1150.

10. **Who fought in the Lincoln County War?**

Two factions of businessmen who used outlaws as their "soldiers" (most notably Billy the Kid) in a protracted battle over the local dry goods trade and lucrative beef contracts. Killings and continued cycles of revenge killings finally climaxed in a four-day gun battle in July 1878.

11. **What New Mexico Indian culture built the famous Gila Cliff Dwellings?**

The Mogollon people, who established their homes high in the canyon walls in the late thirteenth century.

12. **Baseball is the "national sport" of what New Mexico Indian tribe?**

Laguna Pueblo, which has five semi-pro teams and hosts the All-Indian Baseball Tournament every September.

13. What is the Indian Shalako ceremony?

A sacred reenactment by the Zuni in late November or early December of their creation and original migration. The Shalako—giant messengers of the rain gods—come to bless houses specially constructed in their honor and to offer prayers for fertility, long life, prosperity, and happiness. The ceremonies usually continue from one afternoon through to the next and have attracted visitors from around the world, although they have often been closed to outsiders in recent years.

14. Where did Billy the Kid make his New Mexico home?

Mostly in Lincoln County, which he came to as one of the many hired gunmen in the Lincoln County War of 1877-78. He was rumored to have killed twenty-one people during various robberies, gunfights, and jail escapes before Sheriff Pat Garrett finally tracked him down and shot him to death in 1881 in a former army barracks at Fort Sumner.

15. Who were the Buffalo Soldiers?

African-Americans in a segregated Army unit in the late nineteenth century, so called by Plains Indians because of their woolly hair and ferocity. They fought against the Apaches, tried to quell the Lincoln County War, and manned forts throughout New Mexico in the late 1800s.

16. Who were the comancheros?

Mexicans and Americans who traded with the Comanche and other tribes of eastern New Mexico in the late eighteenth and early nineteenth century. Because they often showed little concern for whether their activities were legal or not—bartering guns, stolen livestock, and sometimes kidnapped slaves—they were considered a scourge of the plains by settlers and travelers.

17. What was the Colfax County War?

Conflict lasting through most of the 1870s (with some resistance lingering even longer) between the company that had bought Lucien Maxwell's 1.7-million-acre Miranda-Beaubien Land Grant and the squatters—mostly Hispanic farmers—who had settled there. Hired gunmen, including the notorious Clay Allison, helped the bodies pile up until an estimated two hundred people had been killed.

18. What was Kit Carson's connection to New Mexico?

Taos was his first home after leaving Missouri. After his first wife died and his second, a Cheyenne woman, divorced him, he married Josefa Jaramillo, the daughter of a wealthy Taos family. During this time, he became famous as a guide for expeditions exploring the West, as an Indian fighter, and for his knowledge of the mountain wilderness and its native peoples and animals. He and Josefa are buried near their old home in Taos.

19. Other than the Pueblo Indians, what are the principal native tribes in New Mexico?

The Navajo, Jicarilla Apache, and Mescalero Apache.

20. What member of the New Mexico Rangers, author of the autobiography *A Cowboy Detective*, retired to a ranch outside Santa Fe after twenty years' work as a Pinkerton undercover operative?

Charles A. Siringo.

21. What former dentist was a saloon keeper in Las Vegas, New Mexico, before launching the gunfighting career that made him famous?

Doc Holliday, who killed his first victim at the saloon in 1879. The next year, he joined his friend Wyatt Earp in Tombstone, Arizona, where the "Gunfight at the O.K. Corral" helped make his reputation.

22. The all-Indian parade for what major gathering bans mechanized floats and requires all participants to walk, be on horseback, or ride in a wagon?

The annual Inter-Tribal Ceremonial in Gallup, which also features displays of Indian arts and crafts, competitive dancing, and all-Indian professional rodeos.

23. Who are the Diné?

The Southwestern natives often referred to as "Navajo" by others. "Diné," meaning "The People," is the name they use for themselves.

24. What is a Great House?

Any of the major sites at Chaco Canyon containing buildings with many rooms and kivas. The architectural accomplishments there are considered to mark the peak of Anasazi culture. Pueblo Bonito, one of the largest of these, had more than six hundred rooms arranged on multistory levels.

25. What New Mexico outlaw who later became a policeman fought in the Lincoln County War as part of Billy the Kid's gang while at the same time joining the Lincoln County Mounted Rifles, which Governor Lew Wallace had formed to try to stop the "war"?

Jose Chavez y Chavez.

26. The claims to fame of what Bloomfield, New Mexico, outlaw included shooting a barber to death for accidentally cutting him and turning in a member of his own gang for the $4,000 reward?

Ike Stockton, leader of the notorious Stockton Gang of cattle rustlers during the 1880s.

27. What are Pueblo Indian canes?

"Rods of office" given by Don Juan de Oñate to Pueblo chiefs in recognition of their authority. The custom of the canes as the symbol of their office continued even when the tribes were given the right to select their own leaders without interference from the Spanish. After the American occupation, President Lincoln gave ebony canes with silver handles to the Pueblo governors in 1863, which were designated as "Lincoln" canes.

28. Who were the Code Talkers?

A group of thirty-two Navajo recruited by the Marines during World War II to develop an undecipherable code based on their native language. Because of the language's complex grammar and syntax, and its extremely limited use except on the tribe's reservation, the code could not be broken and played a major role in U.S. victories in the Pacific Theater.

29. What happened to the last seventeen survivors at Pecos Pueblo?

They joined Jemez Pueblo after drought, famine, and disease led to evacuation of Pecos in 1838. The Pecos culture was integrated into that of Jemez, and in 1936, an act of Congress merged both cultural groups into one. A lieutenant governor of Jemez Pueblo still is considered the governor of the Pueblo of Pecos.

30. Why was "Dangerous Dan" Tucker considered more dangerous than better-known lawmen like Wyatt Earp and Wild Bill Hickock?

Probably because of his policy of shoot first and don't bother asking questions. During his years as a deputy sheriff and marshal in Silver City, he noticeably reduced the local crime rate, aided by the widespread fear his quick trigger finger instilled.

31. **What New Mexico gunman was also noted as a knife-fighter and leader of lynch mobs?**

Clay Allison, who led the lynchers of a multiple murderer being held in the Elizabethtown jail (whom he later beheaded) as well as a man in Cimarron who was suspected of killing a Methodist circuit rider. Although he was fast with a gun, and didn't hesitate to use it, much of Allison's reputation was built on his success in man-to-man knife fights.

32. **Who was Hoodoo Brown?**

The leader of the Dodge City Gang in Las Vegas, New Mexico—described by the curator of the city's Rough Rider Museum as "the baddest cowboy of them all." As justice of the peace, coroner, and mayor in 1879 and '80, he recruited several gunfighters from Kansas to be the local police force but led them as well in killings, stagecoach and train robberies, and other thefts, using their official positions to cover up the crimes.

33. **Where do native weavers come together every month in an elementary school gymnasium for the nation's premier auction of contemporary Navajo rugs?**

Crownpoint, New Mexico, about sixty miles from Gallup or Grants.

34. **What is the Gathering of Nations?**

The largest native powwow, held every April in Albuquerque and attended by representatives of more than five hundred tribes. It features more than three thousand singers, dancers, and drummers as well as the Miss Indian World pageant.

35. **What New Mexico cattle baron was a leader of the ranchers who hired Billy the Kid to fight in the Lincoln County War and later had Billy turn against him in a dispute over wages?**

John Chisum.

36. **Who was Hastiin Klah?**

A Navajo singer and medicine man who worked with Mary Cabot Wheelwright to establish in 1937 what is now the Wheelwright Museum of the American Indian. Beginning with the idea of creating a permanent record of Klah's and other singers' ritual knowledge, their efforts led to what became the Museum of Navajo Ceremonial Art. As the Navajo Nation took more control of its religious teachings in the 1970s, the museum changed focus to its current extensive collection of Native American arts.

37. **What was the Butterfield Stage Trail?**

The route through New Mexico carrying mail from St. Louis to San Francisco in the years before the Civil War. (Passengers could ride along also for $200 each.) Because the goal was always to cover the twenty-eight hundred miles in twenty-five days or less, there were never any stops except for a quick change of horses.

38. At what Indian reservation did Coronado's search for the famed "Seven Cities of Cibola" come to an end?

Zuni, where he realized after conquering the Pueblo in 1540 that the stories of fabled wealth that had spurred his and other expeditions from Mexico actually were all lies.

39. What happened to the residents of Chaco Canyon?

They moved away, mostly in the years from 1130 to 1190, but why remains a mystery. The cause cited most often is drought which made it impossible to feed the people who lived there, possibly abetted by a buildup of alkali in the soil due to overfarming. The residents dispersed, some going to the Hopi mesas, others to establish Pueblos at Zuni, Acoma, and other points south and east. Some even went as far as the former Toltec trading community of Casas Grandes in northern Mexico.

40. What Apache war chief born in New Mexico was the last leader of his people's battles with the U.S. government?

Geronimo, who was born in 1829 in what is now Catron County and died eighty years later as a prisoner at Fort Sill, Oklahoma. In between, he led his warriors in many raids, battles, and escapes, principally against Mexican forces but also with U.S. troops after the Southwest became part of the United States. In his later years, he became a celebrity, making public appearances and even riding in Theodore Roosevelt's presidential inaugural parade in 1905.

41. Where in New Mexico were Geronimo and Billy the Kid both imprisoned (though not at the same time)?

Fort Union.

42. What is a hogan?

The traditional Navajo home commonly built of logs and mud, or sometimes of rocks. It is usually round but can be six- or eight-sided, with a door that always faces east and a central air vent in the ceiling.

43. What was the only New Mexico pueblo not to participate in the Pueblo Revolt?

Isleta, most of whose residents either fled to Hopi settlements in Arizona or followed the retreating Spanish to El Paso.

44. How many New Mexico tribes have gambling casinos?

Fourteen: the Navajo, Mescalero Apache, Jicarilla Apache, and Pueblos of Sandia, San Felipe, Laguna, Ohkay Owingeh, Pojoaque, Tesuque, Isleta, Santa Clara, Taos, Acoma, and Santa Ana.

Arts and Entertainment

1. **What two-time Pulitzer Prize winner was both a graduate of and the librarian of the New Mexico Military Institute?**

Paul Horgan.

2. **What famous artist created marionettes for children as well as the head of a huge monster puppet?**

Gustave Baumann, who made the marionettes for plays he wrote about New Mexico's cultural heritage, and, in 1924, made the original head for Zozobra, who gets burned every year for Fiesta de Santa Fe.

3. **What famous native of Roswell decided he'd rather be named after a city in Colorado?**

John Denver, born in Roswell in 1943, who was John Dutschendorf Jr. long before he wrote such hits as "Leaving on a Jet Plane," "Take Me Home, Country Roads," and "Rocky Mountain High."

4. What noted novelist and poet, one of the original winners of the MacArthur Fellowship, has focused on her Laguna Pueblo ancestry in writing of the clashing of cultures and the conflict between the traditional and modern worlds?

Leslie Marmon Silko.

5. What Santa Fe poet and social figure held "teas" attended by such diverse luminaries as D.H. Lawrence, Robert Frost, Mabel Dodge Luhan, and J. Robert Oppenheimer?

Witter Bynner.

6. What Santa Fe sculptor is most noted for her monumental installations and memorials?

Glenna Goodacre.

7. The song telling you to "Get your kicks on Route 66" mentions only one New Mexico city. What is it?

Gallup.

8. What theater production uses simple plots and stereotypes in an annual spoof of New Mexico politics and current events?

The Fiesta Melodrama, staged in Santa Fe late every summer.

9. What Pulitzer Prize-winning newspaperman from Albuquerque became famous as a war correspondent whose columns and dispatches have been compiled into four books?

Ernie Pyle.

10. What work of art in western New Mexico consists of four hundred stainless steel poles in a huge rectangular grid?

The Lightning Field, by sculptor Walter De Maria.

11. Where in New Mexico did such musical greats as Buddy Holly, Roy Orbison, and Waylon Jennings record some of their early hits?

The Norman Petty Studios in Clovis.

12. Who was New Mexico's first published poet?

Gaspar Pérez de Villagrá, an army captain among the colonists traveling with Don Juan de Oñate whose "La História de Nuevo México," an epic poem celebrating Oñate's achievements, was published in Spain in 1610.

13. What New Mexico museum focuses on experiencing the area's Native American, Hispanic, and pioneer cultures?

The Hubbard Museum of the American West in Ruidoso Downs, which originated as the Museum of the Horse.

14. **What natural event in a town five miles north of Española became the subject of a famous work of art?**

Moonrise, Hernandez, New Mexico, taken by Ansel Adams in 1941 and often described as the world's best known photograph.

15. **What novel set largely at Jemez Pueblo won the Pulitzer Prize in 1969?**

House Made of Dawn, by N. Scott Momaday.

16. **Who was the first music teacher in New Mexico?**

Fray Cristóbal de Quiñones, who died in 1609 and had installed an organ at San Felipe Pueblo, where he taught the Indians to sing in Spanish.

17. **What New Mexico city did Bob Dylan write a song about that's included in his famous Basement Tapes?**

Santa Fe.

18. **What writer and anthropologist who lived in Santa Fe for many years won the 1929 Pulitzer Prize and also was a columnist for the *New Mexican* newspaper in Santa Fe?**

Oliver La Farge, author of *Laughing Boy*, who also has a Santa Fe library named in his honor.

19. **What artist noted for his portrayals of life in the Southwest became famous after the landscape and light lured him back to his birthplace in Roswell?**

Peter Hurd.

20. **What was the Taos Society of Artists?**

A cooperative of six Taos artists formed in 1915 who focused much of their work on the daily lives, ceremonies, and customs of the Hispanics and Native Americans of the Taos area. Its members—Joseph Henry Sharp, E. Irving Couse, Oscar E. Berninghaus, W. Herbert Dunton, Ernest Blumenschein, and Bert Phillips—held exhibits in Taos and throughout much of the United States before disbanding in 1927.

21. **Two Navajo police officers solve crimes created by what former New Mexico newspaperman and educator in an award-winning series of mystery novels?**

Tony Hillerman, who wrote eighteen books featuring Lieutenant Joe Leaphorn and Sergeant Jim Chee.

22. **What Santa Fe institution is the largest in the world devoted to its area of artistic focus?**

The Museum of International Folk Art.

23. **What novel about the life of Edith Warner, later made into an opera, tells of her relationship with nearby Pueblo Indians and the scientists making the first atomic bomb?**

The Woman at Otowi Crossing, by Frank Waters.

24. **What noted New Mexico artist turned Santa Fe's first sawmill into his home and studio, a building that now has become a local educational, cultural, and historical center?**

Randall Davey, whose home is the centerpiece of a wildlife sanctuary operated by the National Audubon Society.

25. **Where does the River of Lights flow?**

In Albuquerque, where nearly four hundred displays every Christmas season use millions of lights to blend animated sculptures, cartoon characters, and synchronized music throughout the city's Botanic Garden by the Rio Grande.

26. **What Taos resident created a noted salon in her home in the early 1920s that was often visited by leading artists, writers, activists, and left-wing intellectuals?**

Mabel Dodge Luhan, a longtime radical and wealthy patron of the arts who was married to Taos Pueblo Indian Tony Luhan.

27. **What New Mexico theater founded in 1956 has become world famous for its nontraditional repertoire and high standards of musical excellence?**

The Santa Fe Opera.

28. What famous novel focuses on a Catholic bishop's attempt to establish a diocese in the Territory of New Mexico?

Death Comes for the Archbishop, by Willa Cather, published in 1927.

29. What noted artist first became famous for her paintings of flowers and New York buildings before falling in love with the area around Abiquiu and settling there until she died at age ninety-eight?

Georgia O'Keeffe.

30. What twenty-two-room attraction with walls formed from over fifty thousand glass bottles is filled with carved wooden figures, a miniature Western town, and eccentric collections of Americana?

The Tinkertown Museum in Sandia Park.

31. What southern New Mexico venue features a major touring Broadway, dance, or musical performance an average of every eleven days throughout the year?

The Spencer Theater for the Performing Arts in Ruidoso.

32. Who were the Cinco Pintores?

Five early modernist painters who lived near each other and exhibited together in Santa Fe in the 1920s: Will Shuster, Jozef Bakos, Fremont Ellis, Walter Mruk, and Willard Nash.

33. What successful novelist turned his attention to nonfiction with books based on his experiences as a New Mexico organic farmer?

Stanley Crawford, who described his life on a farm in Dixon, New Mexico, in *A Garlic Testament* and *Mayordomo: Chronicle of an Acequia in Northern New Mexico*.

34. Where can one find more than a hundred galleries within a mile of each other displaying Native American, historic, contemporary, abstract, and Spanish traditional art?

Canyon Road in Santa Fe.

35. What University of New Mexico graduate inspired by the Southwest became noted through his novels and essays as the father of radical environmentalism?

Edward Abbey.

Science and Technology

1. What scientist who became famous in New Mexico was known earlier as the "Coordinator of Rapid Rupture"?

   J. Robert Oppenheimer, so named for his leading role in research at Berkeley before the Manhattan Project on propagation of a fast neutron chain reaction in an atomic bomb.

2. What giant semiconductor maker began business in 1980 on a former Albuquerque sod farm?

   The Intel Corporation, which is now based in California and has thirty-five hundred employees at its main New Mexico site in Rio Rancho.

3. What was Project Y?

   The name originally given to the laboratory established at Los Alamos to build the first atomic bomb. It later was called the Manhattan Project.

4. What New Mexico site is a major center for the study of quasars, supernovas, black holes, and other farflung space phenomena?

   The Very Large Array, a series of twenty-seven radio astronomy antennas that move on tracks across the Plains of San Agustin between Magdalena and Datil.

5. **When was a hydrogen bomb dropped on Albuquerque?**

May 22, 1957, while it was being ferried from Texas to Kirtland Air Force Base. Explanations differ of exactly how the accident occurred during a difficult and awkward pre-landing operation to remove a locking pin that had prevented release of the bomb while in flight. But somehow, the ten-megaton H-bomb—with the explosive power to destroy a city twelve times the size of Hiroshima—pulled free from its mooring and ripped through the closed bomb bay doors. It fell seventeen hundred feet onto a nearly barren mesa owned by the University of New Mexico, killing a lone cow. The twenty-one-ton bomb's conventional explosives, needed to help start a nuclear chain reaction, blew a crater twelve feet deep and twenty-five feet across. Investigators at the scene said no radioactivity was detected beyond the lip of the crater.

6. **When and where was the first rocket launched into outer space?**

February 24, 1949 at the White Sands Proving Ground.

7. **Where in New Mexico is the National Solar Observatory?**

It's ninety two hundred feet high at Sacramento Peak near Sunspot. The facility's instrumentation is available for both day and night viewing.

8. **What New Mexico senator was the last person to set foot on the moon?**

Astronaut and geologist Harrison (Jack) Schmitt, who rode there on Apollo 17 in 1972 and was elected to Congress four years later.

9. **What was the heliograph?**

A wireless solar telegraph that the U.S. Army used in New Mexico in the late 1800s during its campaigns against the Apache and other hostile tribes. The communication network sent Morse code signals over more than a hundred miles of rugged territory via flashes of sunlight reflected by a mirror.

10. **What major discovery did a highway crew make at Blackwater Draw in 1932?**

Artifacts that have made the archeological site near Clovis a model for study of the paleo-Indians who lived there some 11,500 to 13,000 years ago as the last ice age was ending. The findings include arrowheads, scrapers, bone tools, and the remains of mammoths, camels, horses, bison, sloths, and sabertooth tigers. The distinctive points of the Clovis culture have since been found at many other sites in North America.

11. **Why is there a "Golden Cube" in Alamogordo?**

It's the New Mexico Museum of Space History, a five-story building with walls of golden glass which houses, among other attractions, the John P. Stapp Air & Space Park and the International Space Hall of Fame.

12. **How did Fat Man and Little Boy become famous?**

By wiping out two Japanese cities. Little Boy was the code name given the atomic bomb detonated over Hiroshima on August 6, 1945, and Fat Man was exploded over Nagasaki three days later. Models of them are on display in the city where they were conceived, Los Alamos.

13. **Where did Thomas Edison build a plant in 1900 to extract gold from rock and earth with static electricity?**

At Dolores, in the Ortiz Mountains south of Santa Fe. However, his plan didn't work, and he shut down the operation after a few unsuccessful experimental attempts.

14. **What New Mexico location has become a center for the study of archeoastronomy (and what is that anyway)?**

Chaco Culture National Historical Park, where scientists continue to learn about the way ancient peoples understood the heavenly bodies and used that knowledge in their personal and cultural practices.

15. **What are lava ropes?**

A unique volcanic feature (also known as pahoehoe) that's formed as flowing lava cools slightly at the top to the consistency of molasses and then flows over itself into a rope-like shape. They are found in the Valley of Fires north of Alamogordo.

16. **What happened at 109 East Palace Avenue in Santa Fe?**

It was the site of the "depot" that all personnel and shipping passed through during World War II on the way to the secret facility at Los Alamos. As its "gatekeeper," Dorothy McKibbin, recalled: "109 East Palace was an information center, not too accurate but always willing, for inquiries on how and where to get items ranging from horses to hair ribbons. Babies were parked here. Dogs were tied outside. Our trucks delivered baggage, express, and freight to the Hill and even special orders of flowers, hot rolls, baby cribs, and pumpernickel."

17. **Where in New Mexico did archeologists find remains and other evidence of the paleo-Indians who succeeded the Clovis culture?**

Outside the town of Folsom, where in 1925 a cowboy came across the distinctive prehistoric spear points and animal bones that were the first evidence of the Folsom culture hunter-gatherers who lived 9,000 to 10,500 years ago.

18. **Where does the engineering take place to keep the country's nuclear weapons up to date and operational?**

Sandia National Laboratories in Albuquerque.

19. **What New Mexico town bills itself as the carbon dioxide capital of the world?**

Clayton, in the far northeast corner. The carbon dioxide isn't hanging in the air, though, but sits underground, embedded in sandstone southwest of town. It's used in oil drilling and the manufacture of dry ice.

20. **Where in New Mexico is the world's only underground uranium mining museum?**

In Grants.

21. **How did the Trinity Site get its name?**

The Manhattan Project's scientific leader, J. Robert Oppenheimer, said he took it from a poem by John Donne.

22. **What New Mexico astronomer discovered what former planet?**

Clyde Tombaugh, the discoverer of Pluto, who worked at the White Sands Missile Range in the early 1950s and taught at New Mexico State University from 1955-73. He died at age ninety in 1997, and likely would not have been happy to live another nine years and see his 1930 find lose its official status as our solar system's ninth planet.

23. **What New Mexico facility got a big boost in 1992 when the United States decided to stop testing its nuclear weapons?**

Los Alamos National Laboratory, which took over the major scientific job of making sure the country's nuclear arms would still continue working even though they could no longer be tested.

24. **Where is Little Al's Lab?**

At the National Museum of Nuclear Science and History in Albuquerque. The exhibit uses a child-sized robotic puppet of Albert Einstein to help children understand basic concepts of physics.

25. **Where in New Mexico can you find the fastest animal on Earth?**

The Valles Caldera and nearby areas of the Jemez Mountains, home to the peregrine falcon. In their hunting dives after soaring to great heights, these birds can reach speeds of two hundred miles per hour before hitting just one wing of their prey (so as not to be injured by the impact).

26. **Where in New Mexico do you find the greatest concentration of wind power?**

The hundred thirty-six wind turbines, each two hundred ten feet tall, at the New Mexico Wind Energy Center on the plains about twenty miles northeast of Fort Sumner. The electricity it produces can power ninety-four thousand homes.

27. **What do they work on at Los Alamos National Laboratory besides nuclear weapons?**

Lots of things: health, alternative energy, environmental cleanup, supercomputing, and theoretical biology, to name just a few.

28. **What did J. Robert Oppenheimer, the leader of the Manhattan Project, quote from the Bhagavad-Gita when the first atomic bomb was detonated at New Mexico's Trinity Site?**

"Now I am become Death, the destroyer of worlds."

29. **What goes on at the Santa Fe Institute?**

The well-known think tank has brought together researchers from many disciplines since 1984 to study the behavior of "complex systems" in both nature and human activities.

30. **What periods of the geologic timetable are represented in New Mexico?**

All of them. New Mexico is one of the few states with rocks from all four geologic eras: the Precambrian, Paleozoic, Mesozoic, and Cenozoic.

31. **What is the focus of exhibits at the Bradbury Science Museum?**

The history and research of Los Alamos National Laboratory. The museum, founded in 1963, features some forty interactive exhibits and draws nearly eighty thousand visitors a year.

32. **What is trinitite?**

The glassy residue left at Trinity Site from minerals melted by the first atomic explosion there. Little still remains because the site was bulldozed over in 1953, and taking any found there now is illegal.

33. How was the Valles Caldera created?

By a massive volcanic eruption 1.2 million years ago. When it had finished expelling sixty-five cubic miles of ash and pumice, the empty mountain that had held the magma could no longer support the earth above it and collapsed, forming the twelve-mile-wide crater.

34. When did camels roam in New Mexico?

They first showed up in the late Pliocene period 2.5 million to 3 million years ago and hung around for a long time (based on evidence like petrified teeth and poop), finally becoming extinct some ten thousand years ago, about the same time as the related camelids and the mastodons. (Much more recently, camels reappeared in New Mexico shortly before the Civil War when the Army tried using them for desert transportation. But they turned out to scare the horses, and their bad tempers made them tough to manage as well.)

35. Where in Albuquerque are nuclear bombs kept?

At the Kirtland Underground Storage Munitions Complex, at Kirtland Air Force Base. The huge depot, more than three hundred thousand square feet, is the world's largest storage facility for nuclear weapons, and can hold over three thousand nuclear warheads. Nearby Manzano Base had previously been a major nuclear weapons complex tunneled into the Manzano Mountains, and an emergency command post for President Dwight Eisenhower was built into the mountains as well for use in case of a nuclear war.

36. What is the New Mexico Space Academy?

A program of summer science camps for schoolchildren operated in Alamogordo by the Museum of Space History and the International Space Hall of Fame.

37. What prehistoric resident of central New Mexico subsequently came to have his age questioned—and then even his existence?

Sandia Man, who was believed to be twenty thousand to twenty-five thousand years old after well-known archeologist Frank C. Hibben found him (or at least his artifacts) in a cave near Albuquerque in 1940. But other researchers later questioned Hibben's interpretation of the findings, and some even felt that the artifacts had been fraudulently "salted" there to support his theory.

38. Where was the largest solar-heated and -cooled building in the world, dedicated in 1975?

At New Mexico State University in Las Cruces.

39. **Where in New Mexico can you see sand dunes move?**

At White Sands National Monument, the world's largest gypsum dune field. As the wind piles its sand grains higher, the face of the dune gets steeper until gravity pulls an avalanche of sand down the face, moving the dune forward.

40. **How did a boarding school for boys become the site of a scientific project that would change the world?**

When leaders of the Manhattan Project were looking in 1942 for the ideal place to develop the world's first atomic bomb, the winning location was the Los Alamos Ranch School, which Detroit businessman Ashley Pond II had founded in 1918. The factors that convinced them were its combination of isolation, access to water, buildings already in place, and surrounding land largely owned by the federal government.

41. **What New Mexico scientist became wealthy through his invention of the antismoking nicotine patch?**

Frank Etscorn, former dean at the New Mexico Institute of Mining and Technology. When he became nauseous after accidentally spilling liquid nicotine on his arm, the psychopharmacology researcher realized the possibilities for transdermal administration of the drug. And the rest is patent office history.

Mas y Mas
(More and More)

1. **Why are red and yellow the colors of the state flag?**

They were the colors of Queen Isabella I of Castile, in whose name the early Spanish conquistadors explored the American Southwest.

2. **What are genízaros?**

Indians who were taken as slaves by the Spanish in the Southwest, often for household work. By the late eighteenth century, they and their descendants made up nearly one-third of New Mexico's population. In 2007, the state Legislature officially recognized them as indigenous people.

3. **What is the state motto? (And whatever does it mean!)**

The motto is "Crescit eundo," which is Latin for "It grows as it goes." In the original, the Roman poet Lucretius was referring to a lightning bolt's increase in strength as it moves across the sky. (The state also has an official slogan for commerce, business, and industry, adopted in 1975: "Everybody is somebody in New Mexico.")

4. **What was Lew Wallace's "day job" while writing the famous historical novel *Ben-Hur*?**

Governor of New Mexico.

5. **What is the Jornada del Muerto?**

The Spanish conquistadors' name for the most difficult portion of their travel on the Camino Real from central Mexico to Santa Fe. The hundred-mile stretch of desert in southern New Mexico could take up to a week to cross for the earliest Spanish travelers on horseback or foot or in wagons pulled by oxen. The trek's difficulty and danger made "Journey of the Dead Man" a name that fit it well.

6. **What is the oldest continuously inhabited community in the United States?**

The Acoma Pueblo village of Sky City, said to have been constructed in the 1200s high atop a three-hundred-sixty-five-foot mesa about sixty miles west of Albuquerque. Since the three hundred or so buildings on the mesa have no electricity, running water, or sewage disposal, almost all the residents also have homes on the six-hundred-square-mile reservation below. But many still return on weekends and for family visits and religious and cultural occasions.

7. **Why does New Mexico have two state songs?**

One is the official English-language song, "O, Fair New Mexico," and the other is the official Spanish-language song, "Asi Es Nuevo Mejico." (There is also an official state ballad, "Land of Enchantment—New Mexico").

8. **What New Mexico town has the country's only Merchant Marine cemetery?**

Fort Stanton, fifteen miles northeast of Ruidoso. Though it was built to help the Army battle Mescalero Apaches in the mid-1850s, and changed hands twice during the Civil War, the U.S. Public Health Service acquired the military base there in 1899 as a tuberculosis hospital for members of the Merchant Marine, since fresh air and sunshine were the only known "cures" then. Some fifteen hundred patients are buried nearby.

9. **How did a little paper bag get to be the subject of a dispute between Albuquerque and Santa Fe?**

In the beginning were the small bonfires—luminarias—set along the road to guide people to midnight Mass on Christmas Eve. In the early nineteenth century, Chinese paper lanterns, which were easier to use, began to replace them, and then candles in small paper bags came along as a less-expensive, homemade alternative. They were still "luminarias" in Albuquerque, but Santa Feans took to calling them "farolitos"—Spanish for "little lanterns"—and the two cities have gently argued the point ever since. Whatever the name, though, their warmth and glow is a special attraction in both cities, drawing thousands to walk or drive along roads and paths lit by their holiday spirit.

10. What church has built a major facility, including underground tunnels, near the isolated little town of Trementina?

The Scientologist-owned Church of Spiritual Technology, which says the purpose of its Trementina Base is to preserve the writings, films, and recordings of founder L. Ron Hubbard for future generations. The texts have been engraved on stainless steel tablets, encased in titanium capsules, and stored deep in a mountainside. Enormous Scientology symbols, visible only from the air, are reportedly intended to guide future Scientologists to the site when they travel here from elsewhere in the universe.

11. What New Mexico hotel was built by a former chef for Abraham Lincoln?

The St. James Hotel in Cimarron, built by Henri Lambert (who also was a chef for Ulysses Grant). Its famous guests have included Buffalo Bill, Annie Oakley, Wyatt Earp, and Jesse James, and it's reported to still have among its residents the ghosts of several people killed there back in the "wild west" days

12. What violent and deadly event occurred February 2 and 3, 1980?

The riot at the Penitentiary of New Mexico outside Santa Fe in which thirty-three inmates were killed and more than two hundred injured. Despite being brutalized, the twelve guards taken hostage survived. Most of the crimes committed were never punished because fires and other damage in the prison destroyed essential evidence. As a result of the riot, though, the state gradually reformed conditions at the penitentiary.

13. What monument to those who fought in Vietnam was built, in its founder's words, as "an enduring symbol of the tragedy and futility of war"?

Vietnam Veterans Memorial State Park near Angel Fire, whose chapel, its first building, opened in 1971. The idea began with the desire of Victor Westphall to honor the memory of his son and fifteen other Marines killed in a Vietnam War battle in 1968. In addition to the foundation he established, the Disabled American Veterans and the State of New Mexico play major roles in the memorial's operation.

14. What New Mexico governor gave his name to a mountain range, a town, and one of the major native cultures of the Southwest?

Juan Ignacio Flores Mogollon, governor from 1712 to 1715. The mountains were named in his honor, and the name was extended to the prehistoric peoples who were found to have lived there. The town grew up in the mid-nineteenth century around the silver and copper mines that prospered nearby.

15. Who took the Long Walk?

Thousands of Navajo deported from their reservation in Arizona by the U.S. Army from 1864 to 1866 and forced to walk to resettlement at Bosque Redondo near Fort Sumner in eastern New Mexico. Poor crops, limited water and firewood, flooding from the Pecos River, and raids by other Indians made life a constant hardship for the nine thousand Navajo who ended up living there, and in 1868, the tribe was granted 3.5 million acres within its old traditional boundaries. The Navajos began another Long Walk—back home again.

16. What is the origin of the state symbol?

The Zia sun symbol, a circle with rays extending in four directions, was created by anthropologist Harry Mera inspired by a design he saw on a nineteenth-century water jar from Zia Pueblo. In addition to appearing on the state flag, the Zia is the shape of the state Capitol building, known as the Roundhouse.

17. What is the Carlsbad Flume?

A massive concrete aqueduct used to irrigate farmland near the town of Carlsbad with water from the Pecos River. It was built in 1903 to replace a wooden one constructed in 1890 that had washed away a year earlier.

18. **What is the nuttiest town in New Mexico?**

Portales, by a wide margin. The growth and processing of peanuts, along with surrounding dairy farms, supports the small eastern New Mexico city of twelve thousand people. In addition to the principal crop of Valencia nuts, Portales is the country's main producer of organic peanut butter.

19. **According to legend, who were the Indian lovers who gave their name to a busy New Mexico town?**

Tocom and Kari, who together were responsible for the name of Tucumcari Mountain, the flat-topped mesa in eastern New Mexico that the nearby town was named after. It is said that Tocom was killed in a duel with a rival lover, and Kari then took her own life. In an even-less-believable version, the two braves also were fighting to determine who would be the next chief of their tribe, and after Tonopah killed her lover, Kari plunged her knife first into him and then herself.

20. **Where in New Mexico is the country's oldest church?**

It's San Miguel Mission, in Santa Fe. Ground was broken for the chapel in 1610, the year New Mexico's second governor, Don Pedro de Peralta, established La Villa Real de la Santa Fé de San Francisco de Asís, the Royal Town of the Holy Faith of St. Francis of Assisi.

21. **What mountain did Georgia O'Keeffe make so many images of because "God told me if I painted it enough, I could have it"?**

Flat-topped Pedernal near Abiquiu.

22. What mining site that Apaches showed local colonists in 1800 has yielded millions of tons of ore a year since then for its Spanish, Mexican, and American owners?

The Santa Rita copper mine (also known as the Chino Mine) fifteen miles east of Silver City, once the largest open-pit mine in the world.

23. Where did native people in New Mexico create the state's largest art gallery?

Just a few miles northwest of Albuquerque, where nearly twenty thousand pictures were carved over the centuries into a seventeen-mile basalt escarpment that is now Petroglyph National Monument.

24. Who are the penitentes?

A lay confraternity of Hispanic Roman Catholic men that became noted in northern New Mexico and southern Colorado for the members' ascetic practices, which included self-flagellation in private ceremonies at their meeting houses, or moradas. Their full name in Spanish, Los Hermanos de la Fraternidad Piadosa de Nuestro Padre Jesús Nazareno, translates as, "The Brothers of the Pious Fraternity of Our Father Jesus the Nazarene."

25. What is the Blue Hole?

An eighty-one-foot-deep artesian spring east of Santa Rosa that delivers up to three thousand gallons of water per minute. The clear, blue water—at a constant sixty-four degrees—helps the city retain its title of "scuba capital of the Southwest" (though it may not have a great deal of competition).

26. Where is the Cross of the Martyrs, and what does it commemorate?

The white steel cross in Santa Fe is a memorial to twenty-one Franciscan priests killed in the Pueblo Revolt of 1680. A candlelight procession to the cross concludes each year's Fiesta. An older reinforced concrete Cross of the Martyrs a little farther west is barely visible today amid residences and dense foliage, though it can be reached via an old wooden staircase.

27. Who were the "Harvey girls"?

Young women, mostly from the East, who were hired by Fred Harvey to work in his Harvey House restaurants along the route of the Atchison, Topeka & Santa Fe Railway in New Mexico and elsewhere in the West.

28. What New Mexico school was the first in the country to be built totally underground—and why?

Abo Elementary School in Artesia, built at the height of the Cold War, was intended to also function as a fallout shelter if the Soviet Union attacked the United States with nuclear weapons. It was designed to let 2,160 people take cover there (assuming they had all showered recently), and its concrete slab roof was the pupils' playground. Today the former Abo school is used as a storage shed.

29. What branch of the Museum of New Mexico has a "living exhibit" that changes daily?

The Palace of the Governors in Santa Fe, where only American Indians are allowed to sell their arts and crafts under the portal because of a court ruling that the museum's Native American Vendors Program is a "living exhibit."

30. The state song "O, Fair New Mexico" was written by what daughter of the killer of a famous killer?

Elizabeth Garrett, who was born to Pat Garrett four years after he tracked down Billy the Kid. Blind since shortly after birth, she was a friend of Helen Keller and an accomplished musician, and wrote the song in 1915.

31. What is the Bootheel?

The far southwestern corner of New Mexico, named for its shape. Truly a land where no one goes, its fifteen hundred square miles has two roads and one town. But those who can see beauty in the broad, barren plains, rugged mountains, and stark desert scrub will find it there aplenty.

32. **Who are the Matachines?**

Elaborately masked dancers whose ritual drama is enacted by Pueblo Indians on certain saints' days. The dance form, brought to Spain by the Moors and to the New World by the Spanish, is also part of Hispanic culture in several parts of the Southwest.

33. **What internationally recognized architect became a major force for the preservation of historic New Mexico buildings, helped develop Santa Fe Style, and was the official architect of the University of New Mexico?**

John Gaw Meem, who died in 1983 at the age of eighty-eight.

34. **How many states border New Mexico?**

Six: Texas, Oklahoma, Colorado, and Arizona in the U.S., and Sonora and Chihuahua in Mexico.

35. **How did so many different New Mexico Indians get one common name?**

From Spanish explorers who were reminded of their own pueblos, the towns and villages of Mexico, when they found the native peoples along the Rio Grande and elsewhere living in multistory structures built around a central plaza.

36. **What was the famous "Bridal Chamber" in the little town of Lake Valley?**

A silver-lined cave that ended up yielding eighty-six tons of silver. Miners could actually saw off chunks of it in blocks, and a railroad spur was built into the chamber so that the precious metal could be loaded onto ore cars.

37. **What New Mexico mining town had a booming second life built on the slag and refuse of the first?**

Kelly, in the Magdalena Mountains. Silver and lead made it central New Mexico's most prosperous mining town in the 1880s. But after the market crashed in 1893, a mine owner found that the discarded piles of rock contained smithsonite, a type of zinc carbonate used to make paint. The Sherwin-Williams company bought the mine, and the population swelled again until the deposits became too difficult to reach in the 1930s.

38. **What and where is the catwalk?**

A steel pathway suspended from the sheer sides of White-water Canyon near Glenwood. (Or at least it was until devastating floods in 2013 washed major parts of it downriver.) Mining led to the first construction in the canyon in the late 1890s when a pipeline was built to supply water powering a mill that processed seventy-five tons of ore a day. Little was done there after the mill closed in 1913, but during the Depression, Civilian Conservation Corps workers built a hanging walkway along the pipeline route, and the Forest Service in 1961 added the steel causeway that later became the Catwalk National Recreation Trail.

39. **What was the only successful rebellion of North American natives against the Europeans who had conquered them?**

The Pueblo Revolt of 1680, in which the many Pueblo villages of New Mexico rose up together to kill four hundred Spanish soldiers and settlers and drive another two thousand down the Rio Grande to El Paso. When the Spanish returned in 1692, their less-severe treatment of the Indians indicated they had learned at least a few lessons from the revolt.

40. What animal native to Africa was intentionally released at White Sands Missile Range but now has herds so big that it's considered an invasive species and legal target for any big game hunter who can avoid the missiles overhead?

The East African oryx.

41. Who were the Anasazi?

This Navajo word meaning "ancient ones" or "ancient enemy" is the name that was given for many years to the ancestors of people now living in the Four Corners region of the Southwest. Today, the term "ancient Puebloans" or "ancestral Puebloans" generally is used instead.

42. What were Hogback and Rattlesnake?

The two oilfields discovered in San Juan County in 1922 that established New Mexico as a major oil-producing state.

About the Author

Marty Gerber has an addiction to New Mexico. His misguided efforts to relocate elsewhere after first moving here in 1979 have always failed.

There was the "detox" he threw himself into north of Seattle, a "rehab" a few years later in California—but always a relapse. Finally, the truth had to be faced: He was hopelessly hooked on that land and sky reaching into forever; the creative energy giving writer, musician, visual artist a shared common language; even the saturation of its cliches like the cultures, the light, the chile.

And the fact that most of his New Mexico years were spent in the newspaper business in Albuquerque and Santa Fe certainly didn't help. Instead, they created an even deeper immersion, time in which both work and play kept him digging deeper and learning more about the fascinating state he'd adopted. He's driven its miles, walked its trails, seen its sights, read its histories, visited its museums, eaten and imbibed in big cities, small towns, and much that's in between. He feels blessed that his family shares his love for the state and (mostly) makes a home here as well.

He is also the editor of Terra Nova Books.

About the Illustrator

As a child growing up in Mexico City, Andrea "Ani" Lozano spent many hours drawing and painting her impressions of the colorful traditions of her native land.

Frequent travels to her mother's birthplace in Michigan gave her an awareness of the differences in cultures as well as the similarities among all people. Art and humor have been Andrea's way to bridge the two cultures living within her.

She graduated from Olivet College in Olivet, Michigan, with a B.A. in art, and studied graphic design at Western Michigan University in Kalamazoo. She was honored as "Artist of the Year" by the Michigan Hispanic Caucus in 2002.

She has worn many hats as a freelance graphic designer, gallery owner, portraitist, and Ani Rocks Santa Fe rock painter. Among her customers have been the Detroit Art Institute, the Detroit Chamber Music Society, Cranbrook Schools, and the American Humane Association. She illustrated her great-great grandfather's Civil War letters in a book called "Dear Carrie."

Since moving to New Mexico, Andrea feels she has "arrived home" and is visually stimulated by its beautiful landscapes and diverse people. She teaches high school Spanish and art, shows her work at the Santa Fe Artists Market, and teaches workshops through Santa Fe Creative Tourism.